Thinking Out Loud

KATHLEEN SLEDGE

authorHOUSE®

AuthorHouse™
1663 Liberty Drive
Bloomington, IN 47403
www.authorhouse.com
Phone: 833-262-8899

Published by AuthorHouse 04/27/2021

ISBN: 978-1-6655-2296-0 (sc)
ISBN: 978-1-6655-2302-8 (e)

Library of Congress Control Number: 2021907809

Print information available on the last page.

Any people depicted in stock imagery provided by Getty Images are models,
and such images are being used for illustrative purposes only.
Certain stock imagery © Getty Images.

This book is printed on acid-free paper.

Contents

Dedication

For all my family and friends who continue to love and "prop me up" on all sides when I'm not my best. Thank you!

For Lynette, who always stepped right in at all the right times, for consistently being a great sister and aunt.

For my niece and nephew, Daryl and Adrienne, your presence in my life is immeasurable.

Here's one for Bobbie for ringing my phone and checking on me when I've forgotten to call in a while.

For the two gents I owe my life to who offer so much inspiration in my life. My sons, Chis and Evan, stayed with me that one night, and that made a difference in my still being here. You both know how much I love you!

For Tori and her three gems, Justin, Dorian, and Joelle.

For Chris and his three diamonds, Gabe, Jaiden, and Jordan, and for Evan and his jewel, Ean.

You must know my love for you all. This one is for you!

Preface

To those who know me and know me well, my family, and the very few I call close friends, this effort is as much for you as it is for me.

And to those of you who do not know me, indulge in what you read within these pages. Take it and claim it as if it were yours. Because while reading these poems, you will come to realize that it is just as much yours as it is mine. It is as much about you as it is about me.

Throughout the years of pondering this book, I've wondered why it has taken so long. The answer is simple. Experiences create thoughts. With every experience I think, so now this is the time. Through my experiences, I've deemed myself a master thinker. A reflective genius if you will. You know what they say, "You can't rush genius."

That is why I can finally put closure on a project that has tap-danced on my brain for more than thirty-five years.

To you who truly know me, know my struggles, you also know that I am a survivor. You know also that I can do just about anything once I put my mind to it. You know that it takes a while for me to put my mind to some things. I'll keep waiting for something to happen until the last moment. Then and only then, when my back's against the wall or there are no excuses left, will I take action.

Always waiting—that's Kat. I now know that all that waiting has a name. It's called procrastination.

Yes, I've said it. Thanks to Tori, who said, "Mama, I've heard that for years," when I started talking to her about this ingenious idea I had. She looked me squarely in the face and said, "Ma, just do It."

Now that I've given my inability to act a name (procrastination), I feel obligated to produce my marching orders: just do it!

I am obliged to get into the guts of what I must do. Breathe life into a dying carcass. But I feel I owe an explanation to you—and to myself—about what you will find in the poems and monologues contained in these pages. (See, I still stagger a bit, and I still need a little motivation for giving it its life.)

I relish the day over twenty years ago when I knew exactly what my purpose in life was. The day I truly knew God had blessed me just for this purpose. It's fair to say that I always knew. It was just a matter of discipline. A matter of focus. A matter of going deep within to that quiet place and listening for direction. The guidance always comes.

What made this day of revelation different from all the other days was determination. I would not put off any longer. I would organize the years of writings and finish poems I'd started two, three, or sometimes even ten years earlier. I would not put off putting words on paper.

To be quite honest, I was not sure that I could do it. My childhood memories kept getting in the way. Yes, I can even admit now that I was just scared. Where would the support I need come from? Maybe I was just reaching at a dream. As a young child, I was cautioned not to dream. Dreams were not deferred; they were trampled upon, completely snuffed out. I was made to feel stupid for even having the notion that, yes, maybe I could go to the Olympics. I was motivated, and I had the skills.

But who ever heard of a little black—seventy-five pounds soaking wet—nappy-headed, acne-faced, snotty-nosed, double-toothed, scar-legged (from running through poisoned cotton fields in Mississippi) girl from Forty-third and Vincennes, the heart of the ghetto, being a track star. People would say, "She can run like the wind," and Mama would reply, "Yeah, but that's only good to help her get away from those nasty boys."

"That girl can really fly. That doesn't mean a thing because there's nowhere to fly to." – Mary Alice (grandmother)

"She's quicker than greased lightning," people said, and Grandma would say, "Must be something wrong with that girl. That's why she only races with the older boys."

"You know girls ain't supposed to run like that," Uncle James B. said.

I listened to the negative comments, and after a while, I bought into them. Yet if I knew then what I know now …

I should have just kept on running. I should have run from Forty-third and Vincennes to the Indiana state line. Then just kept on running through Ohio. I could've taken a break before heading straight to Tennessee State University, where the tryouts were being held.

Excuse me, but there I go, thinking out loud.

This book, putting my thoughts into words and words onto paper, will probably be a reach for some to read. I decided to combine my poetry, some thoughts about a lot of things, and other writings I've done for various occasions all within these pages. No doubt it will have you smiling. You, you, and even you may comment, "Kat should have chosen her words a little more carefully." But that will probably be the ones for whom those words strike too close to home.

It may leave you with questions. For others it may provide an answer or two. You will note I've included some dates where relevant, to provide clarity, or as a point of reference.

There are a few people who will scratch their heads and say, "Now what the hell is Kat talking about now?"

But always remember in most cases I'm not talking. I'm just thinking out loud.

Acknowledgments

As I begin this new chapter in my life, I look back over the years, and I remember the struggles. I remember each of you in a special way because you played such important roles in my growth as a human being. This book is an example for you. It is evidence that you can accomplish anything if you truly want it badly enough and keep working and believing.

I'm still pressing toward the mark. I'm not perfect, though I know you all think I am (I'm kidding). Even though I can make meals appear on the table when the cabinets are bare, I'm no magician either.

Life has offered me a few second chances. Some I've acted on, and others I've delayed *because*. That's the word, the one word that's kept me stuck for years. Because I'm your mother, here's what I need to say to you, Tori, my miracle baby. I was told by some genius of a doctor that I would probably never have children. When you came along, I decided that I'd better get all my mothering in. Give it my best shot. Tori got the time and attention because this was likely a one-time deal. And just look at you. I think perhaps I did it right!

Because—there's that word again—I did it so right, God showed me favor. He gave me Chris. I truly believe Chris, my beautiful baby, was born to instill in me what a mother's love is all about and to teach me patience. He was born premature because I had gotten back into my career mode and wasn't taking good care of my pregnant body.

Chris taught me the meaning of caring for someone more than you care for yourself. He was ill for the first three months of his life. He needed surgery, but he needed to be a certain weight before he could have the procedure. And because he was in so much pain, it was hard for him to eat. My love and care for him went beyond any scope of understanding. I'm not surprised that you are so quiet as a young man. You made your fuss almost nonstop the first three months of your life.

Just when I was in the prime of life, or maybe just a little past prime, Evan sneaked in. Evan, my love child. Evan is just Evan. My affectionate one. The kissing and hugging one. Busy, busy, overly excited, the one who keeps me on my toes and make me dig deep into my soul for remedies to his never-ending sources of drama. Nothing that worked for Tori and Chris works for Evan. There is something so warm and loving in his eyes. He is always saying, "I love you, Ma." What stands out most in my mind about Evan? One day while I was going over some dos and don'ts with him as mothers do, Evan stopped me and said, "Mama, I can think with my own brain."

I do not know what God has planned for any of my three gems to do with their lives. I am careful to allow them their experiences and to pursue whatever destiny awaits them. I do not want them looking back and thinking, *Because of Mama, I didn't do this,* or, *I couldn't do that. If not for Mama, I should've, would've, or could've.*

God gave me these three gems. Each one is valuable in their own special way. Priceless. The sunshine in my life. I only hope that I've provided a solid foundation on which they can build their dreams because I'm Mama.

To my oldest and only grandson, Jay. You are so wonderful. When Tori decided to go to Northern Illinois University, I began in my mind to arrange my life around your being with me 24-7. When she told me, "I'm taking Jay with me," all the air went out of my body. Even though I think of you as a son, you think of me as Grandma, and that's the way it's supposed to be.

Fancy That: The Lady Takes a Bow

She

She was born a little female,
tiny baby so soft, so sweet.

She was her parents' second;
ole daddy BoBo raved for weeks.

She came into the world screaming.
She was known to always fret.

She needed so much love as an infant.
As a woman,
Love she demands to get.

Wildflower

She rises slowly in the morning
and washes her face in the sweet dew
that has seeped through her petals
during the warm summer night.

After carefully unfolding her blossoms
that reach out to accept the golden sunlight,
she then captures a bit of nourishment
from the soil bed at her feet.

She spends her day in the open field,
bowing ever so gracefully in the wind,
each part flowing ever so gently
with a precision beyond compare.

She's only a tiny wildflower,
and wildflowers love being free,
with miles of fields as her homeland,
dandelions and daffodils her closest friends.

Wildflowers need no shelter from rain,
and they sometimes venture far from home.
Yet they question not their existence
and return mysteriously year after year.

I once picked some wildflowers
while walking through the fields.
I took them home unselfishly—
a beautiful centerpiece they soon became.

The next morning the beautiful wildflowers
all had sad, bowed heads.
To my surprise, the poor wildflowers
were all so unhappy in my home.

Wildflowers are not accustomed to the bondage
of the kind my centerpiece allowed.
They'll die from suffocation;
they can be neither gathered nor crowded.

They are only happy
when they're allowed to stretch out and grow.
To be free in the wind each day,
never captured, never picked, undisturbed.

Sense of a Woman

Step into my womanhood;
take a good look around.
See the beauty of my color:
sweet cocoa brown.

Touch the velvety covering of my body.
Feel the fires raging within.
Yes, I was born a female.
Come, taste the luscious fruits of sin.

This fruit bears all my beauty;
more fruit I'll come to bear.
My body smells of wildflowers or jasmine
and a hint of coconuts, so rare.

Hear the quiet, intimate beat of my heart
while my soul screams out to you,
Let me be loved!
Let me be loved!
Let me be loved!

Laura Lee

Laura Lee was a pretty black thang,
her eyes dark as a Mississippi night.
She was sassy, confident, always composed.
She walked with her head upright.

Now Laura Lee stopped to talk with folks
about her simple life from time to time.
She made a point, had no qualms about telling them
exactly what was on her mind.

Yeah, Laura Lee was county born;
the southern accent prevailed when she talked.
Strangely, people's comments centered on
her "switching," her "Hollywood walk."

Laura Lee stayed centered, always focused,
not very interested in the things people had to say.
She kept her mind on touching her dreams,
determined to let nothing stand in her way.

You see, Laura Lee knew she had a talent.
No! Why should she settle for less?
She aspired to get out of the country
to become a writer and be one of the best.

The hometown folks say, "Oh, Laura Lee, bless her soul,
is kinda lookin' for a pie in the sky."
She never listened, not even for a minute.
She persevered, kept writing, and set her goals high.

Without a doubt, she knew someday she'd make it.
No small potatoes—she'd do it in a grandiose way.
She spent her time dreaming and writing, praying and writing.
She wrote speeches and intros, preparation for her upcoming day.

She wanted the folks in Mississippi to know without doubt
that she had more than a body to give.
She wanted to prove to herself, her mental capacity,
and show black folks how to live.

The hell with just making ends meet.
She'd tried it, didn't like it; other folks she knew did.
She wanted a life where she made all the calls—
a life of leisure, no five-day, eight-hour gig.

At eighteen, Laura Lee finally left her hometown.
Her home folks were awed and concerned.
They knew she'd be back after falling on her face.
They said, "Hardheaded Laura Lee just gotta learn."

A year or so passed; the folks back home
heard neither hide nor hair from Laura Lee.
Then the Western Union arrived late one Friday night:
Laura Lee was just fine and happy as could be.

The message read, the book Laura wrote
would be published sometime in early fall.
She had started immediately writing her second.
She missed them; please give her love to all.

Ironically, everyone began to rant and rave.
They bragged about Laura Lee's book.
Neighbors said they knew her way back when.
Relatives said they always knew she had what it took.

Yeah, Laura Lee had made her mark,
and between writing, she would sit and recall
had she listened to the folks back home,
she'd have never left home or written her books at all.

Another year passed, and the folks back home started again.
They wondered when her career-chasing days might be ending.
Laura Lee began another dream, and thinking ahead,
she prayed and wrote; she knew this was only the beginning.

Today

Today
>   it's all about me and my top.
>   No! Not you—*me*.
>   My needs,
>   my dreams.
>   There are some things that I need,
>   and there are some things that I just want.

Today
>   it's all about knowing where my bottom has been.
>   It's all about where I'm going and
>   how I'm going to get there.

Today
>   it's not about my many mistakes or the limitations—
>   the should've,
>   the would've, or
>   the could've …

Should've not made such bad decisions.
Would've done things differently
>   if given another chance.
Could've just waited and done nothing at all.
Fate, no doubt, would intervene.

Today
>   it's not about my family or my friends.
>   Their support has been there,
>   but it sometimes seems
>   just when you need someone the most …
>   Anyway, it definitely ain't even about family or friends.

Today

it's not about my many lovers,
past, present, or future—
their many faces,
old, young, wealthy, piss poor;

the ones I've left behind,
the ones whose behinds I should have left early on, or
the ones leaving behind someone just for me.
Really? *(reality check, reality check)*
Always changing faces when I should be changing spaces,
drawing into my life what I think I want,
but rarely, if ever, quite getting what I need.
Then again …

Today

I say it ain't about my lovers!
Excuses are not riding this flight.
I'm leaving them outside the door where I'm going.

Today

I'll say it again:
It's all about me!

I want what I want, and I want it *now*.

I want what I want
        when I want it,
        how I want it,
        each and every time I want it!
No! I'm not being selfish.
(OK, OK, maybe just a little.)

I know the flavor of what I want:
I know its smell,
I know its color
and its dwelling place.

I know how my want is traveling;
it travels on the wings of my spirit ...

I know everything about what I want.
I finally figured it out
all by myself, with help from my control tower.

Today

    it's all about me, and

        my peace.

> Blessed are the peacemakers: for they shall be called the children of God. (Matthew 5:9)

It's all about

    my joy.

> Then he said unto them, Go your way, eat the fat, and drink the sweet, and send portions unto them for whom nothing is prepared: for this day is holy unto our Lord: neither be ye sorry; for the joy of the Lord is your strength. (Nehemiah 8:10)

It's all about

    my righteousness.

> For the righteous Lord loveth righteousness; his countenance doth behold the upright. (Psalm 11:7)

It's all about

    my wisdom.

> Wisdom is the principal thing; therefore get wisdom: and with all thy getting, get understanding. (Proverbs 4:7)

And finally, it's all about

    my spirit.

> But God hath revealed them *(meaning the things he has prepared for all who love him)* unto us by the spirit:

for the Spirit searcheth all things, yea, the deep things of God

[continuing] For what man Knoweth the things of a man, save the Spirit of man which is in him? Even so the things of God Knoweth no man, but the Spirit of God.

[taking wing] Now we have received not the spirit of the worlds, but the spirit which is of God; that we might know the things that are freely given to us of God.

[soaring] Which things also we speak, not in the words which man's wisdom teacheth, but which the Holy Ghost teacheth; comparing spiritual things with spiritual. (Corinthians 2:10–13)

That's right.
So I say finally,
　　　It's all about me and my Spirit.

While Reflecting on Life

I Need a Change

I need a change from this ho-hum life.
I need a moment or two to review my goals
and access my intentions.

I need some time to reckon with myself,
to analyze what I like about me.
I need time to refuel my emotions.

I need a chance to get away from it all,
to examine the course of my life.
I need a chance to figure out exactly what's wrong.

I need to meditate on my past,
gather my thoughts of the future,
rearrange my priorities, put things in
the right perspective.

I need a change from my dreary existence.
I need to run barefoot in the sand,
swim in the open sea,
and lie in the warm, inviting sun.

I need to have a heart-to-heart talk
with myself—and me alone—
to seek out and be totally honest
about my feelings.

I need a change—not tomorrow but *now*.
I need my own space
on which to build my life's foundation.
I need my own playground;
I'd equip it with my own brass ring.

I need a good, nurtured garden to plant ideas.
Together the ideas and potential can grow.
I need to own the sky to guarantee a rainbow
after each of life's storms.

Negative Thoughts

I used to think, in a way,
that to be someone
I must know somebody.
To acquire a few riches and fame,
I must know of gold mines undiscovered.
And to go anywhere in life,
I must own my own plane.

I used to think, sort of,
that in order to better myself,
first I'd have to move to the suburbs.
To make it to the top
I'd have to knock friends down.
In any game of chance
odds are I'd lose.

I used to think, kind of,
to feel safe in love, be content,
to find someone who loves me,
in order not to be hurt,
never care.
To really win at love,
make all the rules.

I used to think, truly believe,
if the majority say yes,
it's best not to say nay.
If the wind is blowing to the west,
make my journey due east.
If my goals seem unattainable,
change goals.

I used to think strange, negative things
when I was young, when I was a babe.
My mind foggy with shallow beliefs,
yet not knowing where to find answers.

Now I'm old, and through my many journeys
and experiences, I know.

True, life offers me no guarantees.
But in order to prosper,
I need only to keep trying.

That if I forget my friends
on my uphill climb,
they most certainly will remember me
should I happen to fall.

Now I know …

To feel safe in love,
I must have the capacity to love,
the flexibility to compromise and understand.

If I think the majority is wrong,
there's a chance that I'm right.

And if adverse winds blow,
as they surely will,
I must always continue
in the direction of my goals.

Life's a Bitch

We are in this mess together;
by and large, fair just ain't fair.

We have our ups, but mostly our downs,
things in this world I'd rather leave behind.
'Cause life's a bitch.

Trying to make a little sense of all this,
but people keep changing on me all the time.

What's right for me is out of the question for you.
What I despise is glorious to you.

We see each other through rose-tinted lenses,
never able to distinguish the red from the blue.

I'm giving up trying; damn tired of lying
about things that don't matter to you anyway.
Yes, life's a bitch.

To try to relate what I've been through today
would be like fishing in a dried-up spring.

Explain as I may, tomorrow's another day
with a whole set of problems all its own.

Oh, you may say this broad's experiencing
some malfunction of the brain.

But I'm all sane, trying to figure out the games
you insist on playing with my mind.

The masquerade is not over to most people it seems,
even though their costumes hide not their souls.

It's not for me to get caught up in this
arena of disguise if I can't camouflage the
rest of my life.
Because life can be beautiful.

Heart, Hand, Head

Have faith in yourself that you can achieve.
Every reward in life is yours to receive.
Accomplish one goal, and go on to another.
Reexamine that goal and reach a bit further.
The world is yours, so take a stand.
    The world is yours to command.

Hold on to reality, but also believe in your dreams.
Attack your opposition, no matter how hopeless it seems.
No man can conquer what he's afraid to quest.
Do whatever is necessary to stand the test.

Habituate listening and learning; mix thoroughly with caring.
Establish what's essential in a world that's so demanding.
And last but not least, show others your gains.
Demonstrate most any goal can be obtained.

Man

Can it not be that since the beginning of time
man has been the ultimate power?

The driving force that is quite evident in every
woman, man, and child?

The backbone of generation upon generation
of deed-doers, way-makers?

The moralist judge of every human incident,
our guiding hand that even our children's
children will have to reckon with?

Is it impossible to believe
that man, for life eternally, will be the seer of
all future events?

Man, the healer of almost every human illness.
Man, the answer to the unsolved mysteries
of the world.
Man holds the key to all locked doors.
Man can think, plan his thoughts, and reap
great rewards from his plans.
Man, with the capacity to rise above mere existence
and live in mansions in out-of-the-way places.

Man, who is able to predict the social and financial
statuses of the world's greatest nations.
Man, be he so gifted.

Can he not see that he is not extraordinary
simply because his pigmentation varies?
You being rich, me being poor.
I'm black; you're white. This won't help either of

us live a minute longer than it was intended in
our cycles' beginning.

Looking forward, I see days of harmony and
peace with all men.

Fish of the sea all share the same home.
Birds sing in harmony with other birds.

The trees have a life span all their own.
They stand erect, the willow next to the oak.
The sun and clouds are different; but still,
they can both occupy the sky.

You and I must forget the disguises we are in.
We must learn to communicate from within.

Enjoy the lifespan we each have.
Make a habit of helping man live with man.

We Can

If we can, make one friend each day.
Guide someone who's lost their way.
Reach out and touch a stranger's hand.
Tell our children we understand.

Place a teaspoon of love in our family's cup.
Give words of inspiration; lift spirits up.
Try hard to smile when we want to frown.
Help the less fortunate when they are down.

Make it our purpose to give out joy.
Give strength to some little girl or boy.
Open our hearts, and let love pour in.
Lend a helping hand to a needy friend.

Meet a stranger and extend your hand.
Let him know you're his fellow man.
Whether black or white, that's not our concern.
We can help each other live.
We can help each other learn.

Moments

On any given day,
as we rush to and fro,
it's easy to get caught up in moments.

We move hastily in and out of people's lives.
We count our wins, play down our losses,
and quickly move on to the next experience.

In our quest to be the best,
in our effort to finish all tasks,
we forget to reflect in the moment.

We forget to take a minute.
Stop! Take a deep breath and
slowly, consciously, breathe out.

Inhale slowly.
Accept the fact
we are in the moment for only a moment.

Exhale.
Take some time out.
Others can and will carry on while you rest.

Inhale again slowly.
Stand under the tree of trust
knowing there are some who have your best interests at heart.
Relax.
Allow the gentle breeze of tranquility
to intoxicate and completely sop your senses.

You'll be just fine.
There's no need to be afraid.
Allow yourself to get soaked in peace and tranquility.

Open your big umbrella of understanding.
Let others shower you with their kindness.
Focus as you begin to experience life through their eyes.

Relax as night begins to fall.
Enjoy the stillness knowing
there's always tomorrow.

This Time

All thanks and praise is due to my Lord
for giving me the strength to stretch out in
faith, knowing that there is nothing too hard for God.

A journey of climbing
to the mountaintop, and just when I'm about to breathe the fresh air of tranquility,
I plunge down the mountain, headfirst, hitting rock bottom.

Most times I've had the fortitude and determination to just jump right up and start
the climb all over again. Then, which has been the case most often, I'll just lie at
the bottom of the mountain, not even from exhaustion, because I've never considered not getting up and climbing to the top again.

I question each time as I rest at the bottom, is there a fast, more productive way to
scale the mountain? Or should I be searching for the secret to staying on the top
after a successful climb? No, even though my subconscious mind whispers to me,
Go on, admit it, you just love the thrill of the climb.

I know that there will eventually come the day when these fifty-three years catch up with me,
or I'll just get bored and tire of the climb.

Whatever the circumstances, I know one day real soon I'll master the art of mountain climbing. I'll excel in keeping my footing once I reach the top. No, I won't

timber when I'm halfway up and the wind begins to blow cold and hard.
I'll know that this is my last chance.
This is the final effort.

This time I will have no worry about the jagged edges, the sharp peaks on the
rough side of the mountain that leave my hands raw.

This time I will triumph when my head begins to spin. I'll be victorious because this
time I'll know that I'm not afraid of the climb; nor do I crave the sheer pleasure of
the climb.

I've done it over and over again, and now I realize it's not about the climb at all.

It's about what happens after the climb. I'm poised on top. I've finally made it.

This time once I've reached the top, I'll just sit there on top of my world and let my
feet hang down.

This time, instead of falling to the bottom, I'll just leap from one mountaintop to the
next—
        —to the next.
    This time I'll stay on top.
    This time I won't be afraid of heights.
    This time I'll relax and enjoy the view.

My Country Home

The town is small; the people are few.
The warm air smells of magnolia blossoms and dew.
In the evening the sun sets slowly behind the everglades.
The nights are filled with a distant cricket serenade.

From my window I can watch the moon and stars.
I can count the constellations both near and far.
I see clearly the beauty of the heavens above.
I can sit and dream; I can live and love.

The state of your mind is sinfully carefree.
This must be the way life was meant to be.
No noise or pollution of the city's rat race.
Just hills and streams and wide-open spaces.

Country living seems to complement my very being.
I'm beginning to discover my life's true meaning.
I discovered the secret to relaxing and being free.
To the doors of serenity, I hold the key.

My friends in the city I sure miss a lot.
I hope someday they find what I've already got.
I've found my oasis in this rich southern terrain.
Away from rush hour traffic and subway trains.
Away from uptight people and cries in the night.
Away from junkies and muggers and continuous fright.
If I return to the city, it won't be for long
for I've found happiness in my new country home.

Regarding Love

Love Is

Love is sunshine. Love is rain.
Love is laughter within your pain.

Love is peaceful and outspoken.
Love is deception where there once was devotion.

Love comes in smiling.
Love leaves wearing a frown.

Love can lift you up.
Love will let you down.

Love has a bright side and a dark.
Love is simple; loving is hard.

Love is happy.
Love is blue.

Love is me sometimes loving you.

Web

There was a time in my life,
or shall I say my existence,
when I felt no need to love,
no reason to care or understand.

My mind,
in constant conflict with my emotions,
could not readily distinguish my essential needs
from my selfish wants,
my meaningful purpose from my fate.

I surrendered to this fate.
I suppressed the time element
while standing by all my uncertain convictions.
Consequently, I locked myself away from reality
and spun a web around myself to absorb the hurt.
No one was allowed to come near.

This web was my only solitude.

I somehow convinced myself that someday
fate would change it all.
Just as autumn changes to winter,
and April passes directly into May.
I made all kinds of excuses for the anger I displayed.
I believed, truly believed,
this way of life was meant to be.

Then I met you.

Your smile was warm and penetrating.
You looked at me with eyes so inviting.
I searched for words never spoken.

You touched something deep within me.
I could feel my web slowly falling apart.
You sought to release me from my entrapment,
and I wanted the entanglement no more.

Your unspoken words told me you cared.
My eyes nor my heart could lie.
The pleasure I felt was so unique.
You taught me how to smile.

The emotion is quite real.
Yet I still find it hard to believe
that one man could tear all my defenses down.

You destroyed my web and replaced it with hope.
You erased my fears with a substitute of love.

Now that you've released me,
please stand by me till I'm strong.
I'm still a bit fragile, but I like what I feel.
Stay with me till all traces of the web is gone.

My Private Passion

You are what I think about
when I think about forever.

You are both my spiritual strength,
and admittedly, yes, my physical weakness.

In you I find a warm contentment
for all the little pleasures once denied.

You are my private passion.
You are my perfect place for peace.

Did I ever tell you that,
That you're the reason behind my secret smile?

I guess you should also know
you're exactly what I need yet so cautious to ask for.

You are a visionary,
seeing things in me I'm hiding from other eyes.

You make me want to laugh at life.
You taught me how to smile.

What's that language you speak so fluently?
Oh, so that's the language of love.

What's that crazy thing you do with your eyes?
Yeah, you can even speak the language without saying a word.

Where did you come from,
Loveland, Passion Island, or Blissville?

And where are we going?
To that place where only the two of us can go.

Or to that special, special place.
You know the place, that one place!

The place where you inspire me
and delight me and cause such a stir in my brain.

Is that, too, part of my private passion?
Dancing, singing, rejoicing,
laughing, caring, and finally asking—

Will you always remain my private passion
and
continue to complement my heart?

If

If I've hurt you any, please forgive me.
If I've caused you the tiniest of pain,
the way of life is so uncertain.
Sometimes the whole world seems insane.

If I could show you all the love
I have for you in me,
you would have faith and wait to see
how my life turns out to be.

If I could only touch your hand and perhaps
lay all my troubles at your feet, would
that make you happy? Oh no,
my troubles head-on I must meet.

I keep my problems to myself,
trying to spare you the least little pain.
I'll conquer my problems on my own,
and I'm sorry if I've caused you shame.

Don't worry about me, I beg you please.
I can handle my own life you'll see.
I will be successful in my own right.
I'll be happy as can be.

The people you love seem to hurt you most.
Their aims seem far from what you'd expect.
I'll bring you happiness, no matter the cost.
This is my promise; on this you can bet.

If I could make the whole world happy,
and myself be happy, too,
there would be nothing I'd like more.
There would be nothing I wouldn't do.

I've paid my dues, and yet
more dues I'm expected to pay.
I'm not complaining, oh no.
Just thanking God for another day.

A Place in the Heart

I know a place where cool breeze blow,
tantalizing the shadows of my insecurities
and dancing ever so softly on my fantasy of you.

A place where you and I can go laughing, carefree,
to massage my curiosity in the excitement of you
and bask in the warm misunderstanding of our souls.

This place in the heart where I go to find
the stimulation for all my contemplations of you
and affirmations for all the uncertainty within me.

This place where my once-confused mind
can take a break and be OK with the fact
that the mind is complicated, and thoughts are incomplete.

This place is in the heart.

When I Think of You

When I think about you,
I think of what might have been,
of what could be,
of what really is,
and what will never be.

I think of happy times
and of sad times.
I think of all the things I can't forget
and all the things you can't remember.
I think of times when I want you and you're not here,
and the times I need you and you are.

Whenever I think about you,
I think of how happy I am when I'm with you,
how sad I am when you leave,
how grateful I am knowing you will return,
yet knowing you will always leave again.

When I think about you,
I can visualize you loving me,
though I see the fire in your eyes.
I can still feel the distance and understand
you not wanting to love me
and willing yourself to be indifferent.

When I think about you,
I sense a burning desire
that time may or may not erase.
I sense us merging, one in the spirit,
knowing there are so many obstacles in our way.

When I think about you,

my spirit soars,
my heart palpitates,
my senses take flight,
my passions become aflame,
my reasoning becomes hazy,
my sensibility gives way to my sensuality.
I become totally and captivatingly
rosy-eyed turned blue.

I think of a thousand yesterdays,
I hope for a thousand more tomorrows
whenever I think about you!

I Wish I Knew

I wish I knew how to know you.
At times I really feel that I do.
When you do something so familiar
or say something I knew you'd say
or perhaps say nothing at all.
Just smile in your own special way.

I wish I knew what makes you tick,
what really gets the blood pumping in your veins.
Especially when I'm near you,
and you're not comfortable with my loving care.
Yet when I'm far away,
you express needing me and wanting to share.

I wish I knew just how to love you.
A little bit here and there.
Not giving too much as not to smother.
For sure you'd retreat to safer ground.
Not giving so less that you become certain
that I don't need your love around.

I wish I knew how to understand you
at all times, the way I sometimes do
understand the reason for your distance.
Understand the source of your hurt and pain.
Understand the opening up of your heart to me
allows you to get into "feeling" again.

I wish I knew how to care for you
at a distance that makes you content.
But loving from afar I've never mastered.
I wish I could care for you, but like you,
just be totally indifferent.

Just when I think I have some answers,
just when I feel I'm getting close,
you do something so unpredictable;
you say something I've never heard before.

You make my mind start to question again
if what we have is fantasy or real.
My heart sinks and takes to new heights,
just like a Ferris wheel.

I wish I knew, but since I don't,
you have one of two things to do:

Teach me what I need to know.
Teach me what I ought to do.
Little by little,
one day at a time,
teach me the ways of you.

I'm in no great hurry,
but to stay, I really must know.
Teach me when to slow down,
when to let go.
A spoonful of love here,
a tablespoon of care there.

No doubt I could love you for a lifetime,
but first I must know that it's OK.
I could give you all of me, but
first you must teach me how.
Teach me where you want your love.
Teach me your secret … now.
Tell me when I'm getting close.
Or just simply tell me to go.

You and Me

Somewhere in the revelation of time
our eyes met, and the manifestation
of our love began.

Radiant love
that shown brighter than the brightest star,
beaming with happiness.
A happiness that no words can quite put together.

Glowing with joy, joy for being together.
Joy for just being alive.

A love held firmly with hope.
Hope for tomorrows that are carefree and warm.

Somewhere within the midst of uncertainty,
our hearts stood strong and merged to form
an everlasting chain of desire and devotion.

Circumstances in our way, no matter which
direction we flounder,
jealousy knocking at every door.

Looking opposition squarely in the face,
we held our ground.
The pursuit of happiness is our driving force.

So …
somewhere on some cold lonely night,
while people of the world are filled
with hatred and despair,

there will lie you, with me by your side,
and peace will be our blanket.

I'm in Love

I'm in love,
really in love.
Here's how I know.

I giggle when I get that warm sensation;
you know the one.
That tingling feeling
way down deep whenever we touch.

I even like to play … again!
I dance and I sing.
I dare to say I feel good all over.

Can't think of anyplace I'd rather be
than with you.

What's that? Did I hear you say
you love me too?

I'm so excited at the end of the day.
We lay side by side.
Our love is our haven.

You arms are my shelter.
My breasts your pillow. and
peace our blanket.

Let Me Love You

My love is crying out to you.
Please don't close the door.
Help me find some answers in my life,
answers I'm desperately longing for.

Let me learn to care for you.
Let me hold you when you cry.
Never leave me alone and hurting;
never let us say goodbye.

Let me help you understand me.
In return, I'll try to understand you.
Let us work together, finding happiness
in whatever we set out to do.

I want time to just stand still
until once again we touch.
Let our hearts always remember
the passion we both long for so much.

Let me be your friend and lover,
and comfort you at the end of your day.
Please, just let me love you
for now, for tomorrow, and always.

Dreaming

A dream, what's a dream?
A dream is something you wake up to find
has taken you to another space in time.

A dream?
A dream can seem so real and true that
if it catches you, you might not make it
back to reality.

In my dreams
I dream of me and you, off sailing to
some unknown paradise.
I dream of you, and I quietly vanish
in a warm, love-filled night.

Funny, but my special dreams
have a mysterious way of seeming real.
My dreams make me feel that time
is only a passage through to another world
that I'm sure to find.
Sorne brand-new place that's only yours
and mine.

I dreamt that we took the train of life
to the end of the line.
And we filled each other's years
with a love so divine.

But in real life, our love can easily be
the kind of love that I have to dream to see.

No. Loving and dreaming is no fairy tale.
No Jack and Jill, no farmer in the dell.

And when I wake up someday and finally see
that our love is missing the beauty that
could easily be,

We'll have to find a way
to say goodbye on that day
Because I can't let go of the beauty of
my dreams.

Bondage

Do your thing, and do it good.
I'd do my thing if I only could.

My heart's on fire, but
my mind's in a knot.

My body is eager, yet
my ego is shot.

My head held to the sky
with eyes that want to cry.

Please,
release these chains of bondage,
and let my spirit fly.

Intruder

You really weren't invited into my life;
you just stepped in boldly.
Never asking if it was all right to turn my world
upside down, to change all my plans. and
take my heart.

Admittedly I welcomed the intrusion
without much reservation. I accepted your smile,
so warm and sincere.
Your words were comforting and so
unrehearsed. Your loving: gentle and complete.

My day started and ended with you.
Your smile my wake-up call.
Your touch told the greatest bedtime story.

We laughed at ourselves for taking such a risk.
Yes, we dared to take a change; we both wanted
to feel, really feel love again.
We assured ourselves that fate had unlocked
this door, and God's grace was our key
to enter.

Yes, your entrance was swift
with passion and compassion.
Your retreat was with the same urgency—
minus the compassion.

And I gave myself to you so unselfishly
because …

I believed in you:
    in your hopes and wishes,

in your dreams,
in your ability to make me feel secure,
in your strong determination to supply my needs.

I trusted you:
within my home,
with my children,
as the caretaker of secrets, and
the keeper of my heart.

I loved you:
without reason, and

without reason, you left. Yet I still believe in you—that, for whatever the reason,
you feel that you are doing what's best.

I still love you—whether you want to return that love or not.

And I trust in you—that if I'm wrong about all we had, if it was all just a figment of
my imagination, and that if you are not really ever coming back, that you will return
my heart; I need it to try to love again.

Our Love

Our love,
radiant love.
Shining brighter than the brightest star,
glowing with joy,
held firmly together with faith.

The pursuit of understanding
its driving force.

Rising to new heights,
forming an everlasting chain of devotion.

Yet on those cold, lonely nights,
when criticism, doubt, or jealousy
try to invade our haven,
there will lie you, with me by your side.
and peace will be our blanket.

Meditative Moments

Daily Prayer

I open my eyes to another day.
I fold my hands, and to my Lord I pray:

It is your guiding hand that will watch my moves.
I'm striving hard; I hope you approve.

Your love throughout the world is ringing.
Praises to God I will be singing.

And even if sometimes I am overcome with fear,
I reassure myself that you are near.

Then there are times when my whole world falls down.
But my Bible tells me you can always be found.

Sometimes, oh. Lord, I just need a friend.
Your friendship is there to the very end.

At the close of my day, I thank you again.
Thanks for getting me through another day of sin.

As I lay down my head on my pillow to rest,
I make to you only one last request:

Open my eyes tomorrow once more.
I'll strive to do your will the same as before.

If during the night my name comes around,
I hope to go peacefully, not making a sound.

But if I'm blessed to see another day,
As the day before, I'll start it the same way,

with a prayer of giving thanks to you.
You are my friend; you'll see me through.

Payday

It truly pays to serve the Lord
in and out of season.
It truly pays to serve my God,
even when you must search for a reason.

In the good times and in the bad times,
for his just cause we kneel to pray.
We do not know the time or the hours,
but we do know that soon will come
payday.

Listen to me as I tell you stories,
stories about two men of old.
Great men of faith, of worship, and honor.
Men who served the Lord
instead of idols of gold.

Men like Daniel.
"Daniel, oh, Daniel,"
this says King Darius, Nebuchadnezzar's son.
"Come here, Daniel, come here I say.
Did you hear my decree, yet you pray?

Eat of my meat, and drink of the wine,
or in the den of lions you are sure to stay,
or hear my decree and heed my warning.
Do not kneel three times a day to pray."

But Daniel continued to serve his God,
and a great reward had he.
He had greater vision and the
gift of interpretation.

What about Job? Perfect and
upright man that you are.
Your oxen, your sheep
have all been taken away.
Your children are gone, and your
health is poor.
Yet you shave your head and
fall down to pray.

They say curse the Lord you serve right now
and die; look how your body is shaken.
From where I sit it seems to me
that you, dear Job, have been forsaken.

Job's reply was quite consistent
with how he's always lived.
He believed in his weakest hour
that the Lord had the power
to give.

Job served the Lord in and out of
season, knowing that payday
would bring means to the ending.
God blessed Job's faithfulness three times
more at its end than at the beginning.

It truly pays to serve the Lord.
For his just cause, just kneel and pray.
We do not know the minute
or the hour, but soon will
come payday.

What's Your Price?

Listen to me as I tell a story about a wealthy man of little faith.

I've heard him say on countless occasions that people are fools
to believe in God, that they are feeble to put their faith in things
untouchable and cannot be seen.

One day he even said that he was God,
and all things good in his life came from him.

He said that he had made an abundance of wealth and
that he and he alone had the power to survive.

I looked at this man.
I pitied this man.
For the words he spoke, he did believe.

He ranted, he bragged about the wealth he possessed,
of all the accomplishments he had made.
Before I knew it, I was speaking out loud.
I said boldly to the wealthy man,
"Oh, man of great wealth, can you tell me,
with all your possession beyond compare,
what of the sun that rises in the east each day?
What price did you pay for the sky?
The rain that falls so that flowers can grow.
Tell me what is the price for the air you breathe
or for just waking each and every day?

What price do you pay for happiness and health?
Did you pay one thousand dollars or more
for the stars that shine or the winds that blow?

I've heard you tell of wealth beyond compare.
You've even said that you are king.

But miracles have been known to happen.
Tell me, for the miracle of life, what's your price?

A bundle of gold cannot equal the abundance
of wealth that comes with faith.
When your life's all over and your debts are all paid,
tell me what price tag is on eternal life?

The millions you've saved will be worthless;
your house may crumble down the hill
For hell is the cost of unfaithfulness,
but for the glory of heaven ...

What's your price?"

God's Love

God's love is like an island
in life's ocean, vast and wide,
a peaceful, quiet shelter
from the restless, rising ride.

God's love is like an anchor
when the angry billows roll,
a mooring in the storms of life,
a stronghold for the soul.

God's love is like a fortress,
and we seek protection there
when the waves of tribulation
seem to drown us in despair.

God's love is like a harbor,
where our souls can find sweet rest
from the struggle and the tension
of life's fast and futile quest,

God's love is like a beacon,
burning bright with faith and prayer.
And through the changing scenes of life,
we can find a haven there.

The Fruit of the Spirit

Paul wrote in 2 Corinthians 5:17, "Therefore if any man be in Christ, he is a new creature, old things are passed away, behold, all things are become new."

Paul also told us in Galatians that Christ has set us free. But do you not know that with freedom comes other obligations?

Whether you are young, old, man, or woman, you can meet these obligations. Be set free from all negative emotions and be radiant with the love of Jesus. And yes, you, too, can exemplify "the fruit of the spirit."

Be not misled; exemplifying the fruit of the spirit doesn't just happen. It requires work.

- An astronaut spends hours and hours training before he or she sets off for the moon.
- Likewise, most pianists have to practice untold hours to be able to play Bach without flaw.

Should we do any less than spend hours, days, weeks, and months praying? Even pouring over God's Word before we take those giant steps for God?

We have to work at our vineyard to produce good fruit.

Good spiritual fruit only comes from a well-tended spiritual vineyard by:

1. Staying in God's Word; reading your Bible
2. Staying in a Spirit-filled fellowship
3. Constantly pruning back bad attitudes, cutting off the weak branches of negative emotions
4. Being aware of hurt feelings and allowing God to cleanse those places with the oil of the Holy Ghost.
5. Daily forgiving anyone who has hurt us and praying daily in the Spirit

Earthly vines grow with water, sunshine, and cultivation.
Spiritual fruit grow with praying in the Spirit.

Don't become discouraged if it seems you will never have all the fruit of the Spirit at one time. Just keep striving, keep praying, keep praising, and keep listening. Listen very closely, and you may hear God's work admonishing and reminding you: "You didn't choose me! I chose you! I appointed you to go and produce this fruit always."

So let us go! Produce spiritual fruit!

On the job, produce the lovely fruit of love.
To a neighbor, show the fruit of joy.
Thou wilt keep him in perfect peace whose mind is stayed on thee, the fruit of peace.
Rest in the Lord; wait patiently for him—I say wait. The fruit of long-suffering.

Life is fragile—handle with prayer.
The fruit of gentleness for the children and elders.

A good man produces good deeds from a good heart.
The fruit of goodness.
Now faith is the substance of things hoped for and the evidence of things not seen.
The flawless fruit of faith to move any unwanted obstacle out of your life.

The modest fruit of meekness,
slow to anger, and great in mercy. The well-tempered and very tolerant fruit of temperance.

There's no need to make a lot of noise because,

"We are known by our fruit."

I Am a Woman

I am a woman.
Perfectly carved from the rib of man,
immediately God gave me a purpose on this earth:
to be obedient, to love, and to understand.

I was made just a slight bit more fragile,
and I admit I sometimes even cry.
That's all part of being what I am—a woman.
So is being fruitful; I must multiply.

I am a woman.
As a woman I must strive very hard
to do good in the days I spend on earth
and to always be faithful to God.

I make no claim on being perfect,
but perfection is my highest goal.
But the perfection I seek is not one of simplicity;
it's the perfection of my mind, body, and soul.

I am a woman.
On Christ, the solid rock, I stand.
My Lord, my rock, my salvation.
The King of Kings, the Savior of man.
So I say to the men of the world today,
without you, women are not complete.
I don't want to be above you,
but nor will I be at your feet.

Love, Kindness, Understanding

When I show you a little love,
don't turn cold and walk away.
My love is a priceless treasure.
Its value increases each day. Just hold onto this treasure
for one day love may become extinct.
Then you will be a very rich man
with a gift more valuable than mink.

When I shower you with kindness,
don't be afraid of getting soaking wet.
For kindness will always conquer hostility,
and receiving kindness involves no debt.
The giving and receiving of kindness,
like a fire, it warms the soul.
The rewards you reap from the kindness you sow
will always come triple-fold.

When I offer you understanding,
receive it graciously, and give it back.
Never let skepticism and jealousy
throw you off the right track. Understanding is the foundation
on which all loving relationships must stand.
Understanding balances everyday living
and provides harmony for every man.

This, This, and That

Sistah Monologue

Sistah? Hello? Sistah?
I know you're there.
Can we talk?
I know it's three in the morning.

I know you have a job and I don't.
But sistah, I can't control
when I get my light bulb moments.
Oh, so you think it's just another lonely moment, do ya?

Don't laugh.
We all have our moments.
No! It's not a bunch of BS this time.
But you can call it that if you choose, OK?

Why you laughing and carrying on like that, girl?
Relate to this; let's have a heart to heart.
Better still, a woman-to-woman conversation.
And who knows me better than you?

OK, I heard that muffled sigh, and
I can just imagine your twisted brow.
Yes, damn right!
I'm going through some real funky changes.
(Again?) What you mean, "again"?
Girl, yes there is another brother in my life.
Nope, you're wrong.
He's not the source of all my discontentment.

Well, I'm not you. You know me.
I need to have that other half.
No, I did not say, "better half."
I didn't stutter; I said, "other half."

You know, girl, how I operate, but
truly, this relationship is different.
Go on, and make light of what I'm saying.
I'll just let it run its course.

I know I'm reaching the two-year mark.
Sistah, you're not listening.
It's not time for the two-year recycle plan.
Believe me, I'm through, "fattening frogs for snakes."

Sistah, so you say you've heard all this before.
That's true. But …
this time during my so-called recycle period,
I'm doing something new.

I put myself—mind, body, and soul—into the process.
I've discovered some interesting truths about me.
And I just might use all this new information,
all these truths, to help propel me toward my dreams.

But that's me, my life, and my truths.
What about you?
You can lie there and pretend that you are OK.
Independent woman that you are—been there, done that!

I know that when you went out shopping,
bought that queen-size bed
with your hard-earned, independent cash,
Made a sistah feel real good.

Yet I know that you know that I know
a queen really needs—excuse me—wants a king
to share that space at least sometime.
But that can be our silent little secret.

Please admit at least that!
This is the big girls talking.

Release that little monkey dancing around
in your head.
Whew! Now we can move on.
Come on now, sistah, let's really talk.
You say it's 4:30 in the morning.
I, like you, really still appreciate girls' night on the town.
That bonding thing is really good.

We laugh, talk, and tell a few "good" lies.
Our aim only to make our lives sound exciting,
posturing ourselves to appear a better catch than the next sistah.
There's truly no shame in our game.

During what I called my, "reevaluation period,"
I took some time, stripped my butt to the core.
I looked at me. Soul, naked, bare,
without my many faces. I put all disguises on the shelf.

At this juncture in our lives,
let's examine a few things.
Since we are getting older,
we should, no doubt, be getting better.

No! No! Let me go first.
The first thing I'm ridding myself of is foolish pride.
Sistah, sistah, please listen to me.
I'm talking about the innate idea that I'm superwoman.

I said to me, "You don't have to join the band."
I'm talking about how we—or shall I say me?

Then try extending yourself.
You can stretch a little more, reach, touch.
It's OK, really, trying something different.
Exercise your true spirit; reach out to another.

We come from a lineage of caring, giving, supportive folks.
You'll be just fine; reach out, girl.
I'll be there for you, to catch you if you fall.
You can be there for me to help as I make my climb.

Give it a try. Clear out your mind.
Clean up your heart.
Who told us we had to be cold-hearted to survive?
I'm not riding that train no more.

Finally I understand that the true me needs you.
And I can even have a little love left over for a brother.
I know your needs so well, my sistah,
because you mirror me, and I reflect you.

We only need to pause periodically for reinforcement.
We need refueling at the tank of love.
We need a dip in the pond of hope.
We need to breathe the fresh air of faith.

What you say? OK, but this is important to me.
We can be strong and flex our mental muscles
when there's something to prove; and
just between you and me, I do have a few weaknesses.

At the very core of my weakness are the brothers
and their relationship with the sistahs.
My weakness—the sistahs
and their relationships with their children and the brothers.
We can do this—take all past negative relationships
and use them to our advantage.

The possibilities are limitless; we need only try.
There's enough love to go around.
Damn, you say it's five in the morning.
It's time for you to get up for work.

What you mumbling about now? Say what?
Yes, I'm guilty as charged. The gift of gab?

I know you are relating to all this.
But maybe you were right all the while.
Maybe I am having another lonely moment.
Yes! That's right! I've admitted it.

Sistah, I know it's late or early,
but I really enjoyed the chat.
Especially the part about self-examination.

1.   Brag about how I don't need no brother.
2.   Anything I want I can get myself (that's foolish).

Come on, girl, get real with self. Or can you?
I won't tell if you won't tell.
It's deep; it can be stressful.
Oh, but the beauty of the wisdom …

During the process
I'll keep my warm, caring heart.
You, sistah, please hold on to your level head.
You're gonna need it to separate the haves from the have-nots.

Sistah, think real hard about what I'm saying.
The truth sometimes comes so abruptly.
Especially the truth about self; reckon with it.
Even when it slaps you squarely in the face.

The truth, when you really seek it, will
knock you down on your back,
stand on you, and stare at you
until you understand what it is and its purpose.

I'm a big girl now.
Correction—I'm a grown-ass woman.

I want all my sistahs to grow and stand with me.
Rise to the cause, challenge yourself.
The truth is I didn't call for all that chatter.

I only called to say,
    You are my baby sistah.
    I really love you, girl.
    We needed to air our differences.
    We needed to honor our oneness.
    So glad we tightened up our bond.
    Acknowledged—we still have a ways to go.
    Then and only then can we greet the world, saying,

"Good morning, and have a damn good, happy day."

But initially, I was only calling to say, "Don't forget to drop off my black
shoes."

Black Man

Hey you! Black man,
with your sugar-coated, slick-talking behind.
Open your eyes instead of your mouth. Wise up.
Be on notice, look around; it's a brand-new day.

Us black girls be listening.
You black boys talk kinda loud.
We give less than a damn, ain't the least bit impressed
with your fine ride or your many chicks on the side.

Yes, you, my black brother.
It's time your shaky ego deflates.
It ain't manly and sho nuff not cool,
putting yourself in a position where you constantly take.

I feel you, brother.
But don't always be on the defense.
No, I'm not your—excuse you—I'm not your bitch.
I'm not any of your limited vocabulary names.

We've been whispering behind your back.
We've been laughing while looking straight in your face.
The truth should be told:
You make your black sisters' shame.
You claim to be a superman.
Yet your cape keeps dragging on the ground.
You tell us you can carry your own weight.
But your emotional baggage tends to hold the sisters down.

Get your act together, brother. Today.
Tomorrow is definitely too late.
Sisters are tired of pulling the entire load.
Here's a little secret: Brother, we would welcome a "help mate."

You see, my brother, we really do understand.
Your many trials, yes, you've had to contend with a lot.
What we're baffled about is your seemingly satisfaction
with the little bit you finally got.

Your ambition remains at zero
until you contemplate your next move.
You lose your women during your regrouping,
then blame them for giving you the blues.

Listen to me, black man, I agree with you.
You brothers, yes, you've paid some dues.
Your sisters are right beside—not behind—you,
having your babies, digesting your discontent,
simply being used.

Life is definitely no game. Now you,ve been told.
Second chances are often few.
The hand you are dealt, guess what?
You either play it or you fold.

Life is about living: What about quantum leap?
If we're lucky, it's about loving.
It's about giving and getting ahead.
There's llttle time for complaining and scuffing your feet.

Black man,
now is the time to get in there.
This time, focus, set yourself some goals.

Strive, step over the crap!
If you fall, pick yourself up, refocus,
drive on, think positive, set some additional goals.

Here's another little secret:
Your black sisters love you, man.
Your black sisters want you to succeed.
Your black sisters will have your back.
We'll be there to shelter you from the cold.

A Real Woman

I am woman … a real woman.
A black American woman.
In fact, I am an African American queen.
On occasion—rare
but yes—at certain times, certain folks
will not upset me, and they can and do
get by with calling me "black girl," "soul sister."

Call me a Nubian queen.
And yes, I'll begin to strut,
displaying my rainbow of colors
from the motherland, you know.

Call me an African mother.
Yes, that's right. With pride I'll show my smile.
Other females may act like they don't know,
but I am the original.

It is through me—
and other sisters like me, before me—
that every generation comes to be.
I hold my head high as I display my crown.
My black brothers and black sisters
can always greet me with
"What's up, sistah girl?" I accept their greeting
and acknowledge the compliment.

Relating instantly to the message in the greeting,
I honor their salute.
I know their struggle,
and I know this greeting can only come from the heart.

"Sistah girl" comes from the acknowledgment of the fact
that we share a unique bond,
an adhesion that only evolves
from walking a familiar path in the same shoes.

But:

Don't call me a hussie.
Don't call me a slut.
Don't call me a tackhead or a whore.

Please don't dare call me a bitch.
My mama had a husband,
and besides, she had no relations with a dog.

Whatever you do,
don't ever call me a nigger.
Nigger applies to a condition of the heart.

Don't ever call me a nigger.
Black folks paid with blood, sweat, and tears
to get disenfranchised from the hurt of that word.

Don't call me a nigger because
I just don't like the sound of the word.
There's too much pain and negativity attached.
There's too much hatred, lies told, and hearts broken.

Lives were lost just because of that word,
just the sound of the word.
Oh, what the hell!
Just don't call me nigger because I said so!

Ode to Grandmother

How you have struggled all these years.
The pain in your eyes is all too real.

The happy times are really quite rare,
and my lifestyle seems hard to bare.

You've held our family together through thick and thin.
Now your aging battle you must try to win.

I remember times when you had no shoes.
You won't admit it, but I know you've had the blues.

There are things you do that I don't approve.
I would never interfere; you've paid your dues.

I trust your judgment and wish you'd trust mine.
All bad habits, I long ago left behind.

Let me live my life the way that I choose.
No heartbreak will come; this is my promise to you.

Seeing your smile really touches my soul.
Making you happy is my only goal.

Even if I don't live up to your expectations,
Grandmother you know my love and admiration.

You were a winner since your life's beginning.
I'm also a winner; I'm you all over again.

And one day, Grandmother, just you wait and see.
I'm going to be the granddaughter you want me to be.

I love you, Grandmother, in a very special way,
and to me, each day is Mother's Day.

Thank You, Mama

Thank you for your love for me,
for your caring and devotion.

Thank you for your understanding
when I'm impatient and outspoken.

Thank you for your faith in me
when others doubt my intentions.

Thank you for just being there for me
more times than I can mention.

I thank you for your convictions.
I thank you for your warm heart.

I thank you for your generosity.
I thank you, and I thank God.

Sincerely.

I Remember Christmas

Back on Forty-third Street—
running back and forth to Mrs. Carroll's store.
Twenty-five cents for a pair of earrings, a gift to give—
from upper Morris; that's across King Drive you know.

Mother, cooking in the kitchen.
Potato pie, caramel cake, chicken and dressing too.
Everybody gave everyone something:
Maybe only barrettes, a pair of socks, a hair ribbon (red and blue).

The kids and grown folks got all spruced up
'cause long-lost relatives and friends were gonna stop in.
The dancing and laughter filled the cramped space.
Christmas music and the blues courtesy of Uncle Ben.

We never got a lot for Christmas.
We just looked forward to the gathering of family and friends.
There was enough love and plain ole good times
just being together. I would pray the night wouldn't end.

I've told this same old story to my children;
without the experience, it doesn't have the same appeal.
But then again, they can't relate to being happy with so little.
It's the material things that give them their thrills.

I want all of the family to have a Christmas story
that we can pass on to our children as well.
Their tradition can be Christmas Eve at Kat's house.
Family, friends, food, fun: Oh, what a story they will tell!

We as a family, come on, let's get back to basics.
Come together, enjoy one another; let's laugh and be gay.
Let's celebrate this Christmas Eve together.
Let's do it the old, fun-filled, family way.

I have worked on a special gift to give you.
Take some time for me, our children, our family, and our friends.
It's a gift that comes from my heart.
I give it lovingly. It keeps giving. It'll never end.

I pray you show up this year and next year again.
I want to give you each a gift on Christmas Eve.
I know that it'll make you smile.
I pray it'll warm your heart and give your spirit a lift.

What's the Matter with You

What's the matter with you, girl?
Can't sleep,
can't eat.
Pray.
I've prayed and prayed.

It's 4:17 in the morning.
I think God may even be asleep.
Oh, you say God don't sleep.
Well maybe he's on break.

There's nowhere to go at four in the morning.
No one to call.
Nothing to really do.
The TV's on;
I don't have an inkling what's showing.

I'll just sit up.
Or I can just get up.
Make me a strong cup of French roast, then
I'll just pray—again—
just in case God gets up early too.

I'll call somebody, anybody.
No, they won't understand.
Maybe a cigarette or two or three.
Girl, you really tripping at four o'clock in the morning.

It's Sunday morning; I can prepare for church.
What church?
Any church!
Well at least that's a positive thing.

I know there must be a reason.
I know that there has to be a plan.
It's four o'clock in the morning.
The whole world seems quiet and still.

It's four o'clock Sunday morning.
I'm wide awake.
Coffee done got cold.
Cigarette done burned out.

It's four o'clock Sunday morning.
All's still in my house.
There's nothing to do, no one to talk to.
I'm not happy, yet I'm not sad.

I'm thinking what to do.
God's up; oh, yes he is.
He surrounds my room; I feel his presence
I get it, I feel it: Thank you, Lord,
for waking me up at four o'clock in the morning to write this poem.

Yeah, I hear you thinking,
What took you so long to come to that realization?
Fifty-plus years is a very long time
to figure out that has been you all the time.

All I can say is, "Better late than never."
Trust me, time has not been on my side.
Yet I know a few people today
who still think it's everyone else, not them.

I was at an all-time low.
Yet I still earned this inflated ego.
I finally decided
I was not one of the lucky ones.
You know the ones I'm talking about.

The ones who purchase the winning lottery ticket,
drop a dollar in the slots—instant megamillionaires.
Some old forgotten relative, anonymously gives me millions.
No, I would have to create my own luck.

In my bedroom, with only coins in my pocket
because I had once again made a casino contribution,
my bank account on E.
My supply of tears on full load.

My home in foreclosure.
I drove a car while keeping constant watch for repo men.
The cable turned off. Damn.
A Lifetime movie would be a great escape for now.

Kat's krap—avoiding the inevitable.
Kat's krap—believing I could do nothing.
Miraculous things would just work out.
Kat had stopped praying; God knew already.

I've been here before: same game, different name.
Desperate for money, making decisions out of fear.
Being evicted. On top of all this misery,
To the edge of hell. (Excuse me, Mama, but I've got to be real.)

I began to pray, even surprised myself.
"Lord, please send me someone to love.
Or at the very least, someone to make love to.
There must be someone, somewhere I can call."
Fast-forward to reality.

A noise outside.
A very familiar noise.
Sounds like … Oh, God, it can't be!
The repo man just got my Grand Prix.

Celebrate the Cleansing

Yes! This is the beginning of the rest of my life. This is the future. The vicious cycle of self-destruction ends. I've taken the challenge and completed the awesome process of dissecting, examining, and reconnecting.

I've rearranged all mental activities. No more denial or second-guessing my talents. Oh, yes, I'm ready for the evolution!

I've prepared myself to take ownership of all past screw-ups. The many times when my soul screamed, *Slow down, Take another look, Just step back, breathe deeply, and let your spirit direct you to the place you need to be.*

Yes, for the many times my head said no, yet my busy bottom moved on, not acknowledging the truth. Indeed, I'm to blame for all the unnecessary pain that I've never tried to avoid. For each time I felt the need to succumb to a negative action, my head was always there, defending and trying to protect me. For each time I felt unworthy, for each time I've closed my mind for good, for each time I've rejected a blessing, I take the blame.

I accept the blame today because only after pinpointing the problem can we finally start opening up to a solution.

I'm looking forward, knowing who I am now and what I represent. I no longer allow myself to suffer materially or spiritually. I am one of God's handcrafted vessels, and by virtue of that truth, I owe it to God and myself to stay at a station in life where I can willingly receive his blessings, knowing that all things work together for good.

The plan for my life has already been established. I need only to get in the flow of the plan. Whatsoever is good, whatsoever is fair and of a good report, I think on those things.

- A health body is mine.
- Unconditional love is mine.
- Happiness, joy, peace, and wealth—mine.

I can do anything I choose. I can go anywhere my mind decides to take me. You see, I'm this wonderful creation that has the power to soar above any negative circumstance. I am this glorious creative energy that can simply think on a thing, and through faith, it becomes reality.

Look at me; see my spirit soar. Remember, I am one of God's masterpieces. I am a rare commodity, and it is my duty to be wonderful to myself.

Yes, I accept all the blame for a not-so-clean past. And today, with wisdom and knowledge,
I celebrate with honor the cleansing of my soul.

About the Author

For the author, Kathleen Sledge, every time there was a special event or occasion that required just the "write" words, she was as asked "girl – just put a little something together". She was born in the Delta in Mississippi. She was brought north by her parents as a toddler. She was raised and attended school on the low end of the Southside of Chicago, Illinois.

A born writer, she pulls together dialogue from her experiences as a daughter, sister, mother, and friend. Often she finds herself writing words that most women's inner monologues prohibits them to say—aloud at least. She has a knack for putting words together that cause the reader to relate, reflect, and rejoice.

Over the years, she has grown from having a catering and accommodating personality to being a secure, confident, and mature woman. Her writings reflect this growth, yet she remains warmhearted, focused, and truthful.

After all, these poems were created while thinking out loud.

Kat's Krap

In just one week and one day,
I'll be fifty-one years old.

I looked in the mirror today.
I recognized the image.
It was the same person looking back
who always stared at me before.

Looking at my same old self,
realizing that something wasn't quite right.
The hairstyle had changed,
but I had changed hairstyles before.

The makeup was more natural.
More bronzy, letting my black beauty show.
The eyes, could it be the eyes?
They were softer yet had not completely lost their glare.

Yes, I'd made a great physical change.
I could readily see, upon closer examination,
just maybe catching a glimpse out the corner of my eye.
Peaking right back at me was the same old Kat.

Looking at my physical self, I took a step back.
I tried to convince myself that the mirror was a lie.
I'd spent a lot of time and money on Kathleen,
but the mirror showed me Kat, and her krap.

Kat's krap had me cornered, Kathleen,
holding me hostage for a lifetime of years.
Kathleen was weary from the struggle.
Kat was keeping me from being what I could be.